COOKING THE SOURDOUGH WAY

TIPS, STOVES AND RECIPES

D1028375

COOKING THE SOURDOUGH WAY

TIPS, STOVES AND RECIPES

by

Scott E. Power

ICS BOOKS, INC.

Merrillville, Indiana

Cooking the Sourdough Way
Tips, Stoves and Recipes

recycled paper

All ICS titles are printed on 50% recycled paper from pre-consumer waste. All sheets are processed without using acid.

Published by:
ICS BOOKS, Inc.
1370 E. 86th Place
Merrillville, IN 46410
800-541-7323

Co-Published in Canada by:
VANWELL PUBLISHING LTD.
1 Northrup Crescent
P.O. Box 2131,
St. Catharines, Ontario L2M 6P5.
800-661-6136

Cover Photograph by Tom Todd © 1994
Illustrations by Cliff Moen and James Putrus

Library of Congress Cataloging-in-Publication Data

Power, Scott E., 1970 -
  Cooking the sourdough way: tips, stoves, and recipes / by Scott E. Power.
  p. cm.
  ISBN 1-57034-008-0
  1. Cookery (Sourdough) I. Title.
641.8'15--dc20

94-41249
CIP

Dedication

This book is dedicated to my trip partner and friend Dave Scott,
one of the strongest, most courageous, and sincere people I know.
To Doc Forgey, a fine friend and mentor, who made it all happen,
giving his complete support for this book and the 1991-92 expedition.
To my Family, who love me despite my crazy ways. To my friends,
who love my crazy ways... God bless you all.

Scott Power

Contents

Foreward

Books on sourdough cooking are generally steeped in the lore of the men and women who used it. This book is no exception. But the story told by the young man who wrote it is exceptional. A year after high school he traveled to the far north, 900 miles above the US border, to a remote part of Manitoba. There he lived with a boy his age for an entire year, cut off from all communication with the outside world, living in a log cabin which they built, and living on sourdough.

This is a book written from experience and from his passion for cooking one of the most delightful items ever to be discovered. Scott's partner, David, wrote a book about their experiences together entitled **Paradise Creek**. In it he describes Scott's particular ability cooking sourdough bread on their woodstove.

"I unloaded the .30-.30 and walked inside. The cabin was illuminated with the hissing light of a Coleman lantern and filled with the fragrance of freshly baked bread. I sliced off a hefty hunk of bread and stuffed it into my mouth. With my mouth full I ran up the rickety ladder and into the loft where I found Scott reading a copy of Jack London's classic tale THE SEA WOLF. I nearly died from suffocation for I was out of breath with a nose still clogged with mosquitos and a mouth packed with bread. At last I swallowed the bread and took a deep breath. Scott simply peered down at me over his nose laying his book upon his chest. A rather perplexed look rested on his face and I knew, with my enthusiastic entrance, that I had some explaining to do."

Before I continue I have to say that both Scott and I can bake delicious bread, however Scott is a master. When I was little both my mother and I would make a sandwich, yet for some reason her's always turned out better than mine and her's still do to this very day. It's all in the heart, and after tasting Scott's cabin bread, one comes to the conclusion that he puts a great deal into each and every loaf he bakes.

And Scott puts a great deal of heart into this book.

It's surprising just how important eating, and therefore cooking, is during long wilderness trips. In fact, eating is frequently the single most important topic of conversation. Certain recipes bring with them a story of where they were found, be it on a box purchased in a mining town in Manitoba, given by Mom on a 3 x 5 card, carefully written out for you by the wife of a local acquaintance, or hastily suggested by a bearded surveyor as he climbs back into his helicopter after an impromptu visit.

These stories and others form some of the fabric of this book; the recipes and ingredients most of the rest of it. And then there is Scott's heart. That touch will make this the most unique cooking book in your kitchen.

William Forgey, M.D.
Crown Point, Indiana

WHY
SOURDOUGH?

While taking a walk through the San Francisco airport on January 5, 1989, to pass the time of my six-hour layover, I couldn't help but notice how proud San Francisco is of its sourdough heritage. Every corner I turned seemed to have a colorful display rack with "Genuine San Francisco Sourdough Bread" for sale.

I bought some, yeah sure, a typical tourist ritual. Buy pieces of nostalgia that eventually end up collecting dust on some back room shelf. But, this piece of nostalgia didn't last long enough to collect dust. I ate the bread waiting to board my plane, ruining my appetite for dinner on the flight. So what, I couldn't help myself, I was hungry. Little did I know how important sourdough bread would eventually become to me.

Few people in this world know the sensation of being left alone in an isolated wilderness, to fend for themselves, without civilization. Being "stranded" in a wild terrain to see what it might teach is not something that many people care about doing these days. But, for Dave Scott and me, two friends from Northwest Indiana both twenty years old, it was a dream to see what lessons Mother Nature would teach us if given the chance. So, the dream became a goal: Plan a trip to a remote cabin in sub-arctic Canada and live there to experience all four seasons.

The cabin we sought use of was that of William W. Forgey M.D., the *"Father of Wilderness Medicine"* and author of *Wilderness Medicine*, published by ICS Books. Nestled in the Black Spruce Pines of northern Manitoba, Canada, "Doc" Forgey's cabin was perfect for our dream camping trip. Upon hearing our request, Doc didn't hesitate to grant us permission to use his cabin and from that moment on played a key role in the trip's financial, logistical, and medical aspects and planning.

It took eighteen months to plan our dream, so many details to consider. Twelve months in the north country of Canada, living in a wilderness log cabin, without electricity, plumbing, mail, telecommunications, or medical facilities is not to be treated flippantly.

Sourdough was one of those many critical aspects that we couldn't ignore. It would provide too much nutrition and energy to leave it behind. With it our diets wouldn't suffer. So, on January 29, 1991, a little over two years from the day I had eaten my sourdough bread in the San Francisco airport, Dave Scott and I chartered a single engine "Otter" bushplane on snow skis from Thompson, Manitoba, Canada, to fly us and our sourdough, 180 miles north to Doc Forgey's cabin.

Throughout the Gold Rush of '49, and even as far back as the ancient Egyptians, sourdough has played a helpful part in maintaining a healthy and enjoyable diet. But, only after living in a wilderness log cabin and using sourdough, did I learn how valuable sourdough really is to a backcountry menu.

While living in the boonies, it was immediately obvious by the lack of nearby bakeries and Seven-Elevens, that if we wanted bread we would have to learn how to make it ourselves. Fortunately, we had planned well. We had a sourdough cookbook and "starter" packet complete with a traditional stoneware crock to preserve the sourdough starter. All I had to do was follow the instructions, and everything else would "rise" into place. Wrong.

While reading the sourdough cookbook, I discovered educational, but useless, details about the wheat kernel's three major parts: the endosperm, the embryo, and the bran. Also, I learned that gluten flour is free of starch and is produced from wheat flour which is high in protein. All of these details were fascinating and insightful, but that's all. What I needed were practical, nut-n-bolt details useful for my situation; baking while camping in the backcountry.

Most of the book's instructions were written for the "ideal" home-town kitchen, which was a problem because my circumstances were not ideal. With my wood burning stove, I had no way of maintaining the recommended room temperature of 85 degrees Fahrenheit for any useful length of time. However, the book did give me reference to some delicious recipes that, after working out other tricky details, I was able to transform into epicurean bliss.

Then came March 29, 1991, and the arrival of "Doc" Forgey. "Doc" was more than just the first visitor in three months, he was my second guinea pig after Dave. With Doc I could test the recipes I had been fixing and find out what he thought. Well, I guess he enjoyed the fixin's because consequently he offered me a chance to write this book about sourdough cooking.

Much has been written about sourdough, its folklore and use. My intention with this book is not to add just another card in the "sourdough" subject file-a-deck at your local public library. My purpose is three-fold. One; inform you of the basics to successful sourdough cooking and baking while in the backcountry, where ideal baking circumstances are not found. Two; through knowledge and practice of the basics, help to alleviate the intimidation involved in using sourdough. Three; share some recipes with you that make sourdough cooking so rewarding.

Oh yeah, one more thing. I've tried to be conscientious about not including recipes that call for fancy-smancy ingredients such as kiwi, or multi-colored peppercorns, hemp, or ginseng root. Chances are you wouldn't take that stuff to a campout. But, if you do, great, be sure to experiment and see what happens.

SOURDOUGH GEAR
& SPECIAL INSTRUCTIONS

This book provides you with the basics of successful sourdough cooking and baking while in the backcountry, where ideal cooking circumstances are not found.

In this chapter, I will share with you helpful hints regarding the utensils, ingredients and other special instructions necessary for successful sourdough cooking.

INGREDIENTS

An acquaintance of mine is a professional chef. He has prepared dishes for people such as Ralph Lauren, the popular clothes designer, and George Bush, former President of the United States.

One evening while at a social gathering, this chef and I were talking about the importance of using high quality ingredients. He told me the final product of any recipe is only as good as the lowest quality ingredient, and I agreed. However, in the backcountry high quality ingredients are not always available, unless of course that's what you brought with you. But in my case, while purchasing the groceries for my stay at the cabin, the quantity of supplies was more important than the quality.

So there I was, in my cabin, with mediocre ingredients and the advice of a professional chef which I hadn't followed. However, I did have the one thing that made up for the terrible loss... hunger. When you're hungry in the backcountry, feast upon any of the recipes in this book and I think you'll agree, the finest ingredients couldn't make that much of a difference 'cause it tastes sooooo good!

I've tried to beware of any recipes that called for "fancy-smancy" ingredients that you most likely wouldn't take. For example, pralines, candied cherries, ginseng root, ec hoc genus omne. But let's talk about some of the basic ingredients that are used in the recipes.

Flour

Flour is, besides sourdough which is the leavening agent, one of the most important ingredients. There are many types of flour available on the market, such as wheat, white, "all-purpose", self-rising (not recommended for sourdough cooking), whole wheat, gluten, rye, cornmeal (available in yellow or white), barley, buckwheat, oat, peanut, soy, rice, and potato flour.

Most of the flours listed above are "fancy-smancy" ingredients, and you won't need them for any recipes in this book. The flours called for include white or "all purpose", whole wheat, and rye.

White or All-Purpose Flour

The best white flour to use is unbleached, hard white, wheat. White flour is used most in this book.

All-purpose flour is made from a ground blend combination of hard and soft wheats. Typically, when using all-purpose flour for breads the result is a lighter, moist bread. When using it for cakes, I have found sifting the flour a few times first makes a more "crumbly" cake. I used all-purpose flour in every recipe; it's all I had but it worked very well.

Whole Wheat Flour

Concerning whole wheat flour, the best is whole wheat that has been stone ground. This adds longevity from spoilage and is more nutritious.

Rye Flour

When using rye flour you'll get a more sticky, elastic dough. Also, if you are allergic to wheat flour, rye is an adequate replacement.

A couple more things about flour. When storing it, try to find a cool dry place that's mouse free. In camp, I had delinquent mice who enjoyed vandalizing my flour; you may too. Also, stir your flour before measuring it, to remove any lumps so your measurements are correct. This also eliminates the need to sift.

Leaveners

Now, let's talk about leaveners. There are two main categories: yeasts and chemical leaveners.

Yeast

Yeast, which is more expensive and artificially produced, will not be needed for any recipe in this book. That's because sourdough is the leavener.

Chemical Leaveners

The two most popular chemical leaveners are baking soda and baking powder. These are added to ensure risibility of the bread. However, neither one will increase sourdough's "sour" flavor.

I do give a recipe for Trailblazin' Bannock (see page 24) that you can substitute the sourdough batter with baking powder, if necessary or desired. Replace the 2 cups of batter with 2 Tbs. baking powder and 1 cup of water. You won't have the "sour" flavor, but it does taste good and has been fixed and eaten in the backcountry by campers for decades. As a matter of fact, when I was in the main terminal of the Thompson, Manitoba airport, waiting to board the 1956 single engine Otter bushplane that was taking me to the cabin, a security guard, an older Frenchman, upon hearing where I was going asked me, "Do ya know how to make Bannock?" His question was asked with urgency, the kind that only comes from knowing something someone else needs to know. Happy to see his genuine concern, I replied, "Oh, yes!"

Sweeteners

Sugar affects the action of sourdough, so be careful to add the correct amount. When used in larger amounts, sugar will slow the action of the sourdough. Also, do not use artificial sweeteners because many of them become bitter when the recipe is cooked.

Sweeteners are a fun ingredient though. By substituting one kind for another, you can alter the flavor of your product. For example, try substituting white sugar with brown sugar, molasses, or honey. Each gives your recipe a different taste.

Also, try baking soda as a sweetener for it acts against the acid that puts the "sour" in sourdough. But be careful to add the soda at the very last moment before baking; this helps prevent the leavening characteristics of the soda from affecting the leavening of the sourdough.

Fats

The best fat to use is butter. It can be substituted with an equal amount of margarine or shortening, but they do alter the taste.

UTENSILS

The success of any sourdough recipe depends a great deal on using the correct utensils. However, I understand that when in the woods you don't always have what you need. That's fine, use what you've got. Not using the correct utensils won't completely ruin your product. I just want to offer some guidelines that will help ensure the superiority of your final goodie, that's all.

Containers

The two best containers for your sourdough starter are either the traditional stoneware crock or a plastic container such as products made by Rubbermaid or Tupperware.

Regarding weight and durability, I've found a plastic container is the best. Light and easy to deal with, it won't break when packed. It does, however, lack the sense of antiquity stoneware crock possesses. Whether or not "antiquity" is of any value while in the bush is debatable. I will suggest this: If you do decide to use a stoneware crock, be sure to remove the rubber seal that comes with it. This is so the sourdough can "breathe", and the gases produced by the starter can escape. If you don't remove it, the gases will build up inside the crock until it literally explodes.

Calvin Rutstrum, the famous woodsman, once told a story about a device he made in which to carry his starter. It was designed in the likes of a crock, but he installed a valve on the lid, so that when the gases built up the valve would open, letting the gases escape. Unfortunately, as it was packed away in his Duluth sack, the starter obstructed the valve not allowing it to open. While portaging the pack, a massive explosion knocked Cal off his feet, flat on his face. He said it was as if someone had kicked him in the back with a giant foot. Everything in his pack was covered with sourdough.

When on the trail, possibly the most convenient and hassle free way to carry your sourdough is to take about one half cup of starter and add flour until it's a soft, pliable ball of dough. Generously sprinkle the dough with more flour and put it in a plastic bag filled half way with flour. Seal the bag well and the starter should last a week or two. When you're ready to use it remove the sourdough from the bag and place it in a mixing bowl. Add 2 cups of water, 2 cups of flour, and let it set in a warm place for at least 3 hours, after which it will be ready to use in any recipe.

SPECIAL INSTRUCTIONS

Here are a few special instructions to help you succeed with sourdough:

Do not leave your sourdough in contact with metal for a long time. Aluminum and copper will drastically react with your sourdough and affect its flavor. However, stainless steel utensils are fine to use.

Also, remember, sourdough is a leavener. It can cause your batter to double or triple in bulk. So be sure to use large enough containers to handle the expansion.

Lastly, in regards to the consequential clean-up after the preparation of any sourdough recipe, heed these words: CLEAN DISHES IMMEDIATELY AFTER USE. If you do, you can't go wrong. If you don't, then be warned: There is no accurate means of calculating exactly how many years it may take you to get those dishes clean. It may only take months if you use a hammer and chisel!

SOURDOUGH STARTERS
& RECIPE BATTERS

Before any sourdough recipe can be made, you must obtain a sourdough starter from which the sourdough batter is made. The batter is the leavening agent in your recipe, and is the most important ingredient.

There are two different methods for obtaining the starter. I have found each to work very well. These are commercial starters and self-made starters.

COMMERCIAL STARTERS

Commercially produced starters cost around four to five bucks. They can be purchased through your local grocer or from various camp outfitters.

Typically, commercial starters come in half-ounce packages of dry culture and include instructions on how to prepare the starter. The dry culture is combined with two cups of flour and two cups warm water. After these ingredients are combined, mix with a wooden or plastic spoon. After this, cover your starter container well with a plastic wrap, and let it rest in a warm, not hot, draft-free place for 36 to 48 hours. Depending on the temperature, you may have to give or take a few hours.

During the winter months in the cabin, the temperature was rarely warm enough, long enough to allow the starter to develop. To remedy the problem, I wrapped the starter in extra blankets or something of the like, to keep it insulated. You may need to do the same.

After enough time has passed, the starter should appear bubbly and smell sour. Some have said the sour smell is similar to that of beer. The consistency of the starter will be the same as light pancake batter.

At this point, your commercial starter is ready to use. From it, you can make the primary batter necessary for any sourdough recipe. You will need to keep the starter in a container that will withstand sourdough's properties. See page 7 for complete details. Until you're ready to make the primary batter for a recipe, be sure to store the starter in a cool place.

HOMEMADE STARTERS

If you would rather make your own starter, it's simple to do. Mix two cups of flour with one tablespoon sugar and one-half cake of yeast. Then add warm water and stir until it resembles light pancake batter. Let the mixture set uncovered at room temperature for 36 to 48 hours until it sours. The old woodsman axiom is "the sourer the better." So the longer it sets, the sourer it smells, and the better it will taste. (This is true of commercial starters as well.) The sour effect of homemade starter is dependent upon an appropriate bacterial contamination.

BATTER FOR
SOURDOUGH RECIPES

The starter, as its name implies, is only the beginning. From the starter you will make the key ingredient of all sourdough recipes--the primary batter. Regardless if you're using a commercial or homemade starter, the process for making your primary batter is the same.

The batter will need to be made well in advance of its use, approximately 8-12 hours before. To make the batter, combine $1^1/_2$ cups of starter with $1^1/_2$ cups flour and 1 cup warm water. Add only enough water to make a light batter. Typically, 1 cup warm water works fine, but depending on the flour used, you may need more or less water.

After mixing the ingredients, cover your batter bowl and let it proof in a warm, draft-free area for 8-12 hours. Once the batter has proofed, it will look bubbly and smell sour. At this point it is ready to use. Measure out the amount of primary batter needed for the recipe. Be sure to put any leftovers back into the original starter.

It is a necessity that you rejuvenate your starter to continue living. To do this, simply replace what you took from the starter with the same amount of flour and warm water. For example, if you measured out 1 cup of starter, replace it with 1 cup of flour and 1 cup of warm water. This will help ensure the longevity of your starter, keeping it fresh and useful.

BACKCOUNTRY BAKING METHODS

It was late January 1991, the heart of winter, when Dave and I moved into Doc's wilderness cabin. One of the many joys for me about cabin life is the faithful wood burning stove. Each frigid, winter morning would begin with the building of a fire within the stove. This was done with the fervor of a ceremonial event. Not because of any ritualistic tradition, but in the winter when the morning temperature is 40 degrees below zero Fahrenheit, warmth is the name of the game.

Once burning, the fire was fueled throughout the day. This made cooking and baking extremely convenient. When it came time to try a new sourdough recipe and baking was required, no problem. All I had to do was place my "stove-top oven" on the wood stove, put my dough inside, and let the baking begin. But, as the cold winter season diminished into the warmth of spring and summer, burning the wood stove became less practical, thus did baking on it. The Result: different baking techniques.

Through the writings of professional woodsmen such as Cliff Jacobson, Horace Kephart and Calvin Rutstrum, I learned various cooking and baking techniques. Fortunately, through trial and error I was able to customize these techniques to fit my own circumstances.

How one bakes a recipe in the backcountry depends on a number of variables. First, your environment. You may be in a park where campfires are not permitted. Second, your equipment. You may or may not have a reflector or dutch oven, trail or wood stove. Third, your personal preference and cooking style. The style you feel most competent with will yield the best results for you. Whatever the situation may be, there are still only three main sources of heat for baking in the bush. They are: the campfire, the trail stove, the wood stove, and there are baking techniques that work well for each.

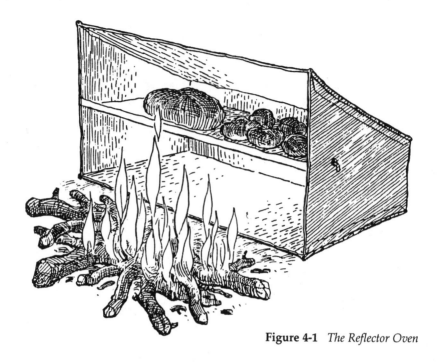

Figure 4-1 *The Reflector Oven*

THE CAMPFIRE

The Reflector Oven

The reflector oven is an excellent way to turn out fine-tasting foods but, the secret of success is not in the oven...it's in the fire! When using a reflector oven, the fire must be high, bright, and hot!

Nowadays, the use of an "open" fire, for much more than roasting marshmallows or telling fireside stories, has diminished and so has the use of reflector ovens. Nevertheless, reflector ovens work well.

When using a reflector oven, set it approximately eight inches away from the fire. Depending on what type of goods you are baking, you may be able to place the dough on the shelf itself, otherwise an appropriate baking tray will be needed. Regardless, make sure to grease whatever you place the bake goods on to help prevent sticking. To ensure the oven is heating and baking evenly, you may need to raise the base of the fire or build the fire upright. Baking times when using a reflector oven are about the same as when baking conventionally. The oven's open face allows visibility and quick access in case of scorching.

Some helpful hints: You'll need a metal spatula with a long handle to maneuver your breads. Also, it is necessary to keep the oven shiny for it to bake properly. BON AMI works well for this.

Reflector ovens can be found at camping stores and/or Boy Scout outfitters. They are also easy to make.

The Skillet Oven—Bannock Baking

"Bannock" is a Scottish Gaelic word for bread that can be cooked on a campfire. Typically, "bannocks" are baked in a skillet.

When baking in a skillet on an open fire, grease the skillet well and spread the dough flat, about an inch thick. When the fire has burned down to a warm bed of coals, set the skillet on top. The baking process is slow, so patience is also a necessary ingredient.

Bake until the down side is golden brown. After which, always shuffle and flip the bannock like a pancake, baking the other side until it is also golden brown. To prevent burning the bannock, you will need to rotate the skillet to bake evenly.

To test for doneness, either thump it with your finger and listen for a hollow sound, or cut a sliver from the middle and taste test it. If it's done, it is best to eat while warm, but bannocks keep well and make great trail snacks. Don't forget to embellish with your favorite topping.

Figure 4-2 *The Skillet Oven*

The Dutch Oven

For decades, dutch ovens were commonplace in homes and "fixed" camps. But cooking with a dutch oven may be a new or even unknown skill for modern day campers.

Fact is, any dutch oven packed for use on the trail will not be convenient. A traditional dutch oven is made of 3/16" thick cast iron and can weigh up to 17 pounds. Its size and weight makes it completely impractical for use on typical camping and canoeing ventures. But there's an alternative, well-modified, dutch oven made of aluminum that has proven to be more useful, lighter, more compact and should not be overlooked.

Figure 4-3 *The Traditional Dutch Oven*

These ovens are excellent for baking, boiling, and the top of the conventional dutch oven makes a great skillet. Look for these dutch ovens at your local camping or Boy Scouts of America outfitter.

An aluminum oven doesn't need to be "seasoned." However, when using a cast iron dutch oven "seasoning" is necessary. Do this by coating the pot with cooking oil, and then bake at 350 degrees for an hour or so.

Although my experience with dutch oven cookery is limited to the aluminum dutch oven, I have found that using a dutch oven is easy, but of course cooking methods depend on your purpose.

To bake: Well seasoned ovens need only a few drops of oil to prevent sticking. After greasing, put dough inside and place the dutch oven on a bed of hot coals. Note: To prevent burning, make sure the bottom of the oven is not directly on the coals, but elevated off of them. If the oven doesn't have legs, elevate it with rocks or cover the coals with ashes to help diffuse the heat. Pile hot coals on top of the oven, too, or maintain a small fire on top. When the main source of heat comes from the top there is a reduced chance of burning the food.

THE TRAIL STOVE

At the cabin there were two trail stoves, and each burned different fuels. One burned kerosene, the other burned white gas. Both worked well for baking.

Having the stoves to experiment with was insightful. With the diminishing use of open campfires for cooking, the popularity and use of trail stoves is great. Thus, it is necessary to be able to use them efficiently and as effectively as possible. Unless you want to burn your buns.

The trail stove baking method I used mostly was a spin-off of a technique called "The Triple-Pan Method." I call my spin-off "The Double-Pan Oven."

The Double-Pan Oven

Place your dough in a well-greased, medium-sized sauce pan. Let the dough proof. Then place the sauce pan with the dough into a large pot. Elevate the sauce pan off the bottom of the pot with small stones. The space created from the elevation prevents burning. Cover the large pot and place it on the stove over low heat. This procedure takes a while to bake but yields good results. It can also be used over the campfire.

Jello Mold Oven

Cliff Jacobson, in his book *Camping Secrets*, describes a technique for trail stove baking called the "Jello Mold Oven." Due to a lack of a Jello mold, I was unable to try this.

In his book, Cliff says, "All you need is a large ring aluminum Jello mold (about three dollars at most discount stores) and a high cover. To use the Jello mold for baking on your stove:

Figure 4-4
The Jello Mold Oven

1. Grease the mold and pour your bake stuff into the outside ring. Decrease the suggested amount of water by up to 25% for faster baking.

2. Bring the stove to its normal operating temperature, then reduce the heat to its lowest possible blue flame setting. Center the Jello mold over the burner head, top it with a high cover (essential to provide room for the bread to rise) and relax. Heat goes up the chimney of the mold, radiates off the cover, and cooks from the top, with no chance of burning.

3. Cool the mold by setting it in a shallow pan of water for a few moments. **IMPORTANT:** Even a light breeze will cause uneven heating of the Jello mold, resulting in a cake that has one side burned and one side raw. So rotate the mold frequently to distribute heat evenly. A windshield of some sort is essential when using a Jello Mold Oven.

Although in this book the topic of cooking is limited to baking only, for complete coverage on cooking in the outdoors, refer to *The Basic Essentials of Cooking in the Outdoors* by Cliff Jacobson, published by ICS Books, Inc.

THE WOOD STOVE

Well, I've saved "wood stove baking" to talk about last because it's so simple and hassle free. It is my favorite method of baking and in my opinion the finest.

For me, this whole adventure in sourdough baking began in my wilderness home, a backwoods cabin. At times, back in "civilization," I experience a thought, sight, or smell, that instantaneously transports my mind back to that pristine place of natural phenomena and timelessness. The retrospection can be triggered by the simplest thing. In this case, it is the thought of "wood stove baking" that has brought a well-spring of memories; the first successful loaf of bread I baked, its smell, its texture, its taste. How one slice alone seemed in itself a meal, but was impossible to stop eating.

What a joy it was to be able to satisfy my insatiable taste buds with my own homemade (cabinmade) bread. What seemed such an impossible task, baking bread, something only grama did, had become my own skill.

If a wood stove is being used, chances are the setting is in a cabin or "fixed" camp. Wood stoves are sometimes designed with an oven compartment in them for baking. If so, great, no instructions are needed except to check your food periodically for burning. With an oven compartment, the baking procedure is rather conventional.

If the wood stove is similar to the one I am accustomed to, the fire burns inside the stove while cooking takes place on the stove's top. If this is the case, using a "stove-top oven" or dutch oven produces good results.

Figure 4-5 *The Stove-Top Oven*

Stove-Top Oven

This method is wonderfully convenient. Just set the oven on top of the wood stove to preheat. Place the bread stuff in its pan inside the oven. Make sure to keep a hot fire going in the wood stove, not an inferno, just hot.

Some stove-top ovens come with a temperature gauge on the outside of the oven. This is handy, but not always accurate. Keep a close eye out so you don't burn your goods.

Stove-top ovens are available through camping outfitters.

The Dutch Oven

The use of the dutch oven was explained in detail previously on page 14. The same rules apply here. The only difference is that you will need to place the dutch oven inside the wood stove, piling hot coals on top. Be careful not to burn the bottom. Remember, elevate the dutch oven off the bottom coals.

SOURDOUGH
APPETIZERS

Recipes include:
- Boonie Bread Sticks
- Pretzels
- Salt Crackers
- Scottish Scones
- Wild Wheat Crackers

One of the funniest times of my stay at the cabin was all about oleo. Oleo? What's oleo, you've never heard of it? Me either. That's what's so funny about February 4th, 1991.

On February 4th, Dave Scott, my partner, found a recipe book full of delicious-sounding recipes. All sorts of goodies such as backwoods lasagna and chocolate cake. Every important backcountry recipe one would want was in this little old recipe book, that suddenly became our hungry bellies' best friend. Dave and I were elated, but there was a problem. All the recipes contained an ingredient we hadn't heard of. The ingredient was called "oleo."

The closest Dave and I had ever come to "oleo" was really "Oreo." "Oreo" cookies that is. It crossed our minds that maybe this was a type-o. Maybe the ingredient was really "Oreo" instead of "oleo." No, that couldn't be it, who would want to put $1/2$ cup of "Oreos" in a dish of Fettuccini Alfredo?

Well, we figured it wasn't a type-o. We looked in the dictionary for a definition, we consulted books that we had available, but not one of them said anything about "oleo." And, being over one hundred miles away from the nearest town, there was no one we could ask.

What to do, what to do?! Theoretically, we could have hiked out on snowshoes, but that wasn't practical for something that might have been a type-o. There we were, with a well-earned hunger, a recipe book of savory foods to feed on, but no "oleo." We decided not to worry about it, and just try to work around it. Besides, we still had other recipes up our collective sleeve. If, and when, we had a visitor from the "outside" we would simply ask them about "oleo." Hopefully, they'd know the answer.

Later that same year on April 9th, we had our first visitor from the "outside," Doc Forgey, our mentor and bearer of current events and nutritional trivia. Among all the things that were on our minds to ask about: How were our families? What about the Persian Gulf War? How were da Chicago Bulls doing? The question with high priority was: What the hell is "oleo?"

"Oleo is an old-fashioned term for margarine," he said, "why do you ask?"

Dave and I just looked at each other, feeling the effect of our youth. We had "oleo" the whole time. Lots of it. It was in the container labeled "butter."

BOONIE BREAD STICKS

(RECIPE YIELDS 30 BREAD STICKS.)

1½ cups primary batter

1 cup hot water

3 Tbs. butter or margarine

3 Tbs. sugar

1 tsp. salt

4 cups flour

Mix ingredients in succession. Add flour slowly, 1/2 cup at a time. Knead dough on flat surface, adding additional flour until dough is elastic. Place dough in a greased plastic container and let set for 2 hours for proofing. After which, roll out to a 1/2 inch thickness. Cut the dough into strips, no wider than one inch. Place onto a greased baking sheet, at least one inch apart from each other. Bake for 20 minutes at 400 degrees or until golden brown.

PRETZELS

(RECIPE YIELDS 15 4-INCH WIDE PRETZELS.)

$1\frac{1}{2}$ cups primary batter

1 cup hot water

3 Tbs. melted butter or margarine

3 Tbs. sugar

$2\frac{1}{2}$ tsp. salt

$5\frac{1}{2}$ cups flour

1 egg or one cup snow

2 Tbs. milk

Mix ingredients in order. Add flour slowly, one half cup at a time. Knead dough on flat surface for about five minutes. Let dough rest for two hours to proof. Break off dough in pieces about the size of a hand ball. Roll each piece into 15 inch lengths and shape them into your favorite pretzel shape. Place onto greased baking sheet or griddle, and set in warm place for 20 to 30 minutes for proofing. Sprinkle with salt and bake at 425 degrees for 15 minutes or until browned. Let cool, then serve.

SALT CRACKERS

(RECIPE YIELDS ABOUT 50 CRACKERS.)

2 Tbs. shortening

2 tsp. salt

$\frac{1}{2}$ cup primary batter

1 cup white flour

Mix ingredients in succession. Knead dough and add some white flour until it just becomes stiff. Roll out very thin and cut out in two-inch squares. Place onto greased baking sheet or griddle. Puncture square with fork and sprinkle with more salt. Bake at 400 degrees for 5 to 10 minutes or until crackers begin to brown. Let cool completely before serving.

SCOTTISH SCONES
(RECIPE YIELDS 10 SCONES.)

1 cup primary batter
2½ Tbs. sugar
½ tsp. salt
1 tsp. baking soda
¼ cup melted butter
1 egg or one cup snow
1 cup white flour

Mix ingredients consecutively. Add flour slowly. Dough should be thick, but easy to work with. The less kneading you do, the flakier the scone. Place a heaping tablespoon of the batter into a hot greased frying pan over medium heat. Cook until brown, then flip and cook other side until brown. Serve hot with butter and jam.

WILD WHEAT CRACKERS
(RECIPE YIELDS ABOUT 75 CRACKERS.)

2 cups whole wheat flour
1 tsp. dill
1 tsp. salt
½ cup shortening
1 cup primary batter

Mix ingredients in order. Knead thoroughly to "bring out" the gluten to make a thinner cracker. Roll dough out on floured board very, very thin. Cut out in two-inch squares and put them on a greased baking sheet or griddle. Puncture squares with fork and bake at 375 degrees for 30 minutes or until brown.

SOURDOUGH BREADS, ROLLS & BISCUITS

Recipes include:
- Trailblazin' Bannock
- Biscuits
- Bread Rolls
- Cheddar Cheese Bread
- Country Cornbread
- English Muffins
- No-Knead Bread
- No-Knead Colonial Bread
- No-Knead Cornmeal-Raisin Bread
- No-Knead Peanut Butter Bread
- Oatmeal Raisin Cakes
- Raisin Muffins
- Scott's Sourdough Cabin Bread

Sourdough bread. Ah, That porous wonder! Not "Wonder" the brand name, but wonder the phenomenon. The kind of wonder that in and of itself is more than meets the eye. For instance, when I make bread I don't just see the culmination of some ingredients thrown together. I see beyond the obvious look for some peanut butter and jelly to spread the porous bread with the blissful pleasure that only comes with PB&J sandwiches.

Bread is much more than the simple sum of its ingredients. Bread is the foundation of the seven epicurean wonders of the world; french toast, grilled cheese, peanut butter and jelly sandwiches, pizza bread, garlic bread, bologna sandwiches, and cinnamon toast. White, wheat, rye, or pumpernickel, it doesn't really matter. All of these gratifying edible delights are only obtainable with bread. Whatever you choose, you'll please your taste buds, and unless you have an allergic reaction, you'll be glad you did.

Life in the backcountry is sometimes rough, but I believe always nurturing, and there is no reason to limit the experience with a diet of "nuts and berries." You need the foundation of the epicurean wonders of the world. You need bread. Forget about trying to pack in store-bought bread, it's a hassle. Besides, it'll never make the trip without getting smashed into bread balls. Impress your trip partners, impress yourself. Bake some bread while in the woods, or the field, and when it's done baking cut a hot slice, spread butter on it, close your eyes, and enjoy. You'll eat till you're full, or until it's all gone, whichever comes first. So don't be an unleavened person, live a full life and celebrate it with sourdough, the superhero of leaveners, the friend of adventurers and prospectors throughout history.

Furthermore, sourdough causes magical things to occur. Things that you don't expect. Things that will cause you to give thanks. A personal experience of this came one day while at the cabin. I was preparing a loaf of sourdough rye bread when I heard the very alluring sound of a flying machine in the distance. I was very excited, hoping it would be someone flying in to visit.

Stopping what I was doing, I rushed outside to look for the plane and the potential visitor. Much to my dismay, it was just a helicopter flying very fast in the western horizon, heading north, to Churchill. Very disappointed, I went back into the cabin to finish baking my bread. A short while later, I heard the sound again, this time very close. Once again, my heart pounded from the possibility of having visitors.

I ran outside and my wishes were granted. This time the helicopter was not far off in the horizon, it was directly above the cabin, so close I could see the eyes of the passengers inside. Startled, yet elated, I waved calmly to appear cautious. Seconds later, the pilot landed the helicopter on the river bank. Out of it jumped a bearded man whom I had never seen. In that intense moment, many questions flooded my mind. Who were they? Why were they here? Where had they come from? Was there trouble? Was this friend or foe?

For the sake of congeniality, I approached the strange man with my hand extended, and we shook hands. The first words spoken by the man rang in my ears as proof of sourdough's magical properties.

"Heard there was a bakery around here," the man exclaimed.

Dumbfounded and relieved, I smiled big and invited them in for fresh baked bread and coffee. For the next hour, we visited, laughed, and they told of current events back in civilization. Arriving as strangers, they left as life long friends.

There's a suggestion for following recipes you may find peculiar. It's the use of snow as a substitute for eggs. This may sound crazy, but it works, and has been used by generations of woodsmen and sourdoughs alike. For every egg called for in a recipe, use one cup of snow. The snow gives the same effect that eggs do, giving the recipe the necessary consistency.

TRAILBLAZIN' BANNOCK
(RECIPE YIELDS ONE LOAF.)

This is the recipe that a wise-looking security guard in the Thompson, Manitoba, Canada airport lobby asked me about. "Do ya know how to make Bannock?" he queried after hearing that I was going to a remote wilderness cabin.

Bannock is superlative for treks, and campouts. It's easy to prepare, no proofing time is necessary, and there is no baking. This bread is fried in a skillet like a pancake. Some call it Skillet Bread.

2 cups primary batter
½ cup butter
1 tsp. salt
1 Tbs. sugar
1 cup flour

Mix dry ingredients, then stir in the batter. Mix well, until dough is like a thick pancake batter. Pour dough into a warm, lightly greased skillet. Fry until done or golden brown on both sides and serve.

BISCUITS
(RECIPE YIELDS 10-15 BISCUITS.)

1½ cups primary batter
1 cup flour
½ tsp. salt
1 Tbs. sugar
¼ cup melted butter

Mix ingredients in order. Pour dough onto a flat, floured surface and knead no more than one minute. The less you knead, the flakier the biscuit. Roll out to a ¹/₂ inch thickness. Using either a cookie cutter or a knife, cut out the biscuits, and place them onto a greased pie pan or baking sheet. Brush the tops with butter. Let set in a warm place for thirty minutes or until double in bulk. After which, bake at 375 degrees for 30 minutes or until golden brown.

BREAD ROLLS
(RECIPE YIELDS 10-15 ROLLS.)

1½ cups primary batter
1 Tbs. sugar
½ tsp. salt
2 Tbs. melted butter
1 egg or cup of snow
2 cups of flour-your choice

Mix ingredients consecutively. Add the flour a bit at a time. Mix until the dough is smooth, then knead dough on a floured flat surface. Add additional flour if needed for elasticity. Place the dough back into a bowl and put in a warm place until double in bulk. Punch down and continue to let set until double in bulk again. Once done, roll dough out to a ¹/₂ inch thickness, and cut into pieces about 3 inches in diameter. Form pieces into rolls, and place them onto a greased baking sheet. Let set for thirty minutes, then bake at 400 degrees for 15-20 minutes or until golden brown.

CHEDDAR CHEESE BREAD
(RECIPE YIELDS ONE LOAF.)

1½ cups primary batter
1 cup milk
¼ cup sugar
1 tsp. salt
3 Tbs. melted butter
1 egg or cup of snow
2 cups grated cheddar cheese
4 cups white flour

Mix ingredients in order. Add the flour a little at a time. Once the ingredients are mixed, turn the dough out onto a flat floured surface and knead it until soft. Form the loaf and place it in a greased bread pan. Let the bread set in a warm place until double in bulk. Bake at 375 degrees for thirty minutes or until golden brown. Test for doneness by thumping the loaf with your finger and listen for a hollow sound. When it's done, remove the bread from the pan and let it cool.

COUNTRY CORNBREAD
(RECIPE YIELDS ONE LOAF.)

1½ cups primary batter
1½ cups yellow cornmeal
1 cup milk
2 eggs or cups of snow
2 Tbs. sugar
½ cup melted butter
½ tsp. salt

Stir ingredients together and pour the batter into a greased bread pan. Bake at 450 degrees for 25 minutes or until golden brown. This bread is only complete when served hot with lots of butter.

ENGLISH MUFFINS
(RECIPE YIELDS 10 MUFFINS.)

1½ cups primary batter
1½ cups flour
1 Tbs. sugar
½ tsp. salt

Mix ingredients in succession. Knead the dough on a flat, floured surface until the dough is easy to handle without being sticky. Roll the dough out to a thickness of a 1/2 inch. Using a knife or cookie cutter, cut out the muffins. Put each muffin onto a greased baking sheet about an inch apart, sprinkle with cornmeal. Let rest in a warm place for an hour to proof. Cook the muffins for 10 minutes on each side in a greased frying pan. Serve hot or let cool to be eaten later.

NO-KNEAD BREAD
(RECIPE YIELDS ONE LOAF.)

1½ cups primary batter
½ cup milk
1 tsp. salt
2 Tbs. sugar
2 Tbs. cooking oil or shortening
3 cups flour

Mix dry ingredients first, then add the batter. Mix well. Once dough is mixed, form a loaf or just pour the dough into a greased pan. Bake immediately until golden brown or test for doneness by thumping the loaf with your finger. If you hear a hollow sound the bread is done. Remove the bread from the pan and let cool.

NO-KNEAD COLONIAL BREAD
(RECIPE YIELDS ONE LOAF.)

1½ cups primary batter
½ cup milk
1 Tbs. sugar
½ tsp. salt
½ cup raisins
½ cup nuts
1½ cups flour

Mix dry ingredients first, then add the batter. Mix well. Allow dough to stay soft. Pour dough into a greased pan, cover, and let set in a warm place for an hour. Bake for one hour or until done.

NO-KNEAD CORNMEAL-RAISIN BREAD
(RECIPE YIELDS 2 LOAVES.)

3 cups primary batter
¼ cup melted shortening
1½ cups milk
¾ cup brown sugar
2 tsp. salt
2 eggs or cups of snow
2 tsp. cinnamon
1½ cups yellow cornmeal
4 cups white flour
2 cups raisins

Mix ingredients successively, but slowly. Be sure to add the flour a little at a time, stirring after each addition. Mix until the batter is stiff. Put in a warm place for two hours to proof or until double in bulk. After proofing is done, stir the batter again. Place the batter into two greased bread pans, and let proof again until double in bulk. Bake at 375 degrees for 45 minutes or until golden brown. When done remove loaves from pans to cool.

NO-KNEAD PEANUT BUTTER BREAD

(RECIPE YIELDS ONE LOAF.)

$1\frac{1}{2}$ cups primary batter

$\frac{1}{2}$ cup brown sugar

$\frac{1}{2}$ cup milk

$\frac{3}{4}$ cup melted peanut butter

$\frac{1}{2}$ tsp. salt

2 Tbs. melted butter

$2\frac{1}{2}$ cups wheat flour

Mix ingredients in succession. Add the flour a little at a time. Once mixed, pour the batter into the bread pan and let set in a warm place for thirty minutes. After which, bake at 350 degrees for 45 minutes or until done. Remove the loaf from the pan and let cool.

OATMEAL RAISIN CAKES

(RECIPE YIELDS 6 CAKES.)

1 cup primary batter

2 Tbs. sugar

$\frac{1}{2}$ tsp. salt

$\frac{1}{4}$ cup melted butter

2 eggs or cups of snow

$\frac{1}{2}$ cup raisins

1 cup oats-rolled or minute, whatever you've got

$\frac{3}{4}$ cup white flour

Mix ingredients well. Knead dough on a flat, floured surface until dough holds together. Divide the dough into six pieces or cakes. Place them on a greased baking sheet and let set in a warm place for an hour. Before baking cut slits in the top each cake. Bake at 400 degrees for 20 minutes or until brown. Best when served warm.

RAISIN MUFFINS

(RECIPE YIELDS 8-12 MUFFINS.)

1½ cups primary batter
1½ cups flour
3 Tbs. brown sugar
½ tsp. salt
¼ cup shortening
1 egg or cup of snow
1 cup raisins

Mix ingredients in order. The dough should be moist and lumpy. Place the dough into a greased muffin pan with cups and let rest in a warm place for proofing until double in bulk. Bake at 400 degrees for 25 minutes or until done.

SCOTT'S SOURDOUGH CABIN BREAD

(RECIPE YIELDS TWO LOAVES.)

Below you will find the recipe that got me this job. This bread recipe became an icon of survival and a Hungertown favorite. Typically, I made white bread, among others, at least three times a week. Good ol' white bread seemed to become the quickest and most favorite to fix.

The recipe got its name for very obvious reasons. It didn't seem fair to limit its name to "Sourdough Bread." How boring, and besides too many cabins, both past and present, have been fed from the sourdough crock to leave out the word "cabin" from its name.

3 cups primary batter
2 Tbs. melted butter
⅓ cup sugar
1 tsp. salt
2½ cups white or all-purpose flour

Mix dry ingredients first, then add the batter. Mix well. Pour dough onto a floured surface and knead the dough with your hands. Once dough is consistently elastic, form your loaf by rolling it up, adding flour if needed, in layers like a jelly roll. Place loaf in greased bread pan. Set in a warm place for two hours or till double in bulk. After proofing period, bake at 400 degrees for 30 minutes until golden brown, or test for doneness by thumping the loaf with your finger. If you hear a hollow sound, the bread is done.

SOURDOUGH
DESSERTS

Recipes include:
- Bite-Size Peanut Butter Cookies
- "Bakers" Chocolate Cake
- Dazzelin' Daves' French Quarter Benyeas
- Mrs. Welburn's Oatmeal Raisin Cookies
- Robin Hood Oatmeal Pudding
- Saturday Morning Cinnamon Rolls

The whole concept of a "dessert" has increased pleasure while in the woods. Many factors come together to help transcend what would be a typical dessert in any domestic environment, into a rapturous experience while in the woods. This happens because of an earned hunger from physical exertion, gratification from the dish's preparation, and having a sweet tooth. Everyone has a sweet tooth regardless of how successfully they disguise it. It is quite a natural tendency and sheer bliss to feed one's appetite for sweets while sitting within a campfire's hypnotic glow. Have you ever met anyone who would *naturally* prefer ginseng root tea over chocolate milk, broccoli over strawberries, a "guru-chew" over candy bars, puffed rice patties over freshly baked chocolate chip cookies? I seriously doubt it.

When in the backcountry few things instigate selfish behavior amongst campers like dessert time. "Are you gonna eat that?" or "Can I lick the bowl?" or "That's all I get?!" These questions come up a lot at campouts during dessert time. Whether or not they are spoken is unimportant. The fact is, everyone's at least thinking it. Rightfully so. Not only is it natural to have an epicurean inclination towards sweets, but after hiking fifteen miles or canoeing for eight hours, it's a damn right! So exercise your right and try the following sourdough dessert recipes.

The desserts I recommend are Dazzelin' Daves' French Quarter Benyeas, Mrs. Welburn's Oatmeal Raisin Cookies, and "Bakers" Chocolate Cake. Each of these desserts has more than just flavor in its favor. Each dessert has traveled large distances to be here between the covers.

Dazzelin' Dave's recipe, created during our stay at the cabin, was a labor of love by my partner to create humanity's finest munchie food, The Dave Perignon of Pastries. Indeed he did just that. I want to go on record and say that "Dazzelin' Daves' French Quarter Benyeas" are the ultimate munchie food. Dave couldn't make enough of these. Each time he'd make them, we would eat them all in one day. Dave always tried to make more the "next time" so they would last, but it would not suffice. We ate them too. Dave's Benyeas are so good that once we started eating them we really couldn't quit. I doubt you'll be able to stop either.

The second recipe came via the polar bear capital of the world, Churchill, Manitoba, Canada from the Welburn homestead, who were kind enough to put us up in their cabin one night when our canoe trip was stranded by a storm and sickness. Throughout the night my innate sweet tooth wouldn't let me get enough of Mrs. Welburn's oatmeal cookies. To help my insatiable hunger, she gave me the recipe.

"Bakers" Chocolate Cake is called such because in our remote cabin location the only chocolate we had to choose from was what we had purchased in Winnipeg weeks before, Bakers Chocolate. We didn't let the lack of variety squander our enthusiasm for the final product...chocolate cake. We used the Bakers Chocolate with pride for having it, and conservation, for there was only a short supply at hand and no stores nearby to replenish it. Each time we ate a chocolate square for "candy," we knew in our minds that it would cost us a piece of cake. But conversely, we knew that making a chocolate cake would cost us candy. Such is life with limited resources. Our gratification demanded sacrifice, and our taste buds demanded nothing less. So take heed, yours may too.

So you see, these are not just your typical "sum-of-the ingredients" recipes. These recipes have a life of their own, a tale to tell, wisdom within, and flavorful delight to share.

BITE-SIZE PEANUT BUTTER COOKIES
(RECIPE YIELDS 4 DOZEN COOKIES.)

½ cup soft butter
1 cup brown sugar
½ cup peanut butter
1 beaten egg
1 cup primary batter
½ tsp. salt
½ tsp. baking soda
¾ cup white flour

Mix ingredients in order. Drop batter by the spoonful onto a greased baking sheet. Bake at 375 degrees for 12-15 minutes or until golden brown. Cool on a wire rack if possible.

"BAKERS" CHOCOLATE CAKE
(RECIPE YIELDS 1 TWO-LAYER CHOCOLATE CAKE.)

½ cup cocoa or chocolate
1 tsp. baking soda
1 cup boiling water
½ cup butter
½ cup shortening
2 cups sugar
3 beaten eggs
1 tsp. vanilla
1 tsp. salt
½ cup milk
1½ cups primary batter
1 cup flour

Mix the first three ingredients and let set for 20 minutes. Then add the eggs, vanilla, and salt. Beat mixture together. Then add the milk, primary batter, and flour mixing well. Pour the batter into a Jello mold or cake pan and bake at 350 degrees for 30 minutes or until done. Remove from pans and let cool on wire racks if possible.

DAZZELIN' DAVE'S
FRENCH QUARTER BENYEAS
(RECIPE YIELDS ABOUT 20 BENYEAS.)

1½ cups primary batter
1 beaten egg
¼ tsp. vanilla
¼ cup milk
2 Tbs. cooking oil
2 cups flour
¼ tsp. baking soda
¼ cup sugar
¾ tsp. salt

Mix ingredients in a large bowl, adding the flour 1/2 cup at a time. Mix well. Place dough onto a flat, floured surface and knead until dough firms up, but is soft and easy to manage. Roll out the dough to a 1/2 inch thickness. Using a cookie cutter or whatever will work, (I used a metal ring from a roll of bandaging tape in the medical kit) cut out the benyeas. Place them on a lightly floured or greased flat surface and set in a warm place for 30 minutes to proof. Meanwhile, in a large bowl mix...

2 cups confectionery sugar
1 cup brown sugar
¼ cup cinnamon

This is your powder coating for the benyeas. As the dough continues to proof, prepare a skillet or dutch oven with cooking oil and heat until it's super hot. Then when the benyeas are done proofing, place a couple at a time in the grease to fry. Fry on both sides until the benyea is brown and puffed up like a doughnut without a hole. When done frying, remove the benyeas from the grease and place in the cinnamon and sugar mixture for coating. Roll the benyea around in the powder to cover the whole benyea. Repeat process until all benyeas are done. These are best served while warm and with coffee. Feel free to experiment, add raisins or cinnamon to the dough for a different variation.

MRS. WELBURN'S OATMEAL RAISIN COOKIES
(RECIPE YIELDS 3 DOZEN COOKIES, DEPENDING ON THE SIZE.)

1½ cups primary batter
1 cup shortening
1 cup white sugar
¼ cup brown sugar
1 egg or cup of snow
¼ cup milk
1 tsp. salt
1 tsp. cinnamon
3 cups oats, minute or rolled

Mix ingredients in order, stirring after each addition. Drop batter by the spoonful onto a greased baking sheet. Bake at 400 degrees for 12-15 minutes, or until done.

ROBIN HOOD OATMEAL PUDDING
(RECIPE YIELDS 5 SERVINGS.)

1 cup primary batter
¾ cup sugar
¾ tsp. salt
1 tsp. baking soda
1 tsp. cinnamon
1 cup minute oats
¾ cup chopped dates
3 Tbs. butter
1½ tsp. vanilla
½ cup honey

Mix ingredients in consecutive order in a large bowl (except the honey). Mix well. Grease a 1 quart bowl or 1 pound coffee can and pour the batter inside. Cover the batter tightly with wax paper or tin foil. Place the pudding bowl inside a pan of boiling water, but be sure to elevate the pudding up off the bottom of the pan somehow. A rack will work or putting stones on the bottom works well. The water in the pan should reach half way up the pudding container. Cover the pan of boiling water and let steam for 90 minutes. When done, remove pudding out onto a serving plate. Cover with honey and serve.

SATURDAY MORNING CINNAMON ROLLS
(RECIPE YIELDS 14 ROLLS.)

1½ cups primary batter

¼ tsp. vanilla

¾ cup milk

¼ cup sugar

1 Tbs. cinnamon

1 Tbs. melted butter

1 tsp. salt

2 cups flour

Mix ingredients, adding the flour a 1/2 cup at a time. Knead dough on a flat, floured surface until smooth and soft. Place dough in a large container for two hours to proof or double in bulk. Turn dough out onto a floured board and roll to a 1/2 inch thickness.

Brush dough with additional butter and sprinkle liberally with an additional 1/4 cup of sugar and 1 tsp. cinnamon mixed together. Roll dough into a cylinder. Brush with melted butter and sprinkle again with sugar and cinnamon mixture, then cut the cylinder into equal sections or rolls. Place the rolls onto a greased baking sheet, cover, and let set in a warm place for thirty minutes to proof. Then uncover and bake at 325 degrees for 25-30 minutes or until done. If possible, let cool on a wire rack. Cover with butter and honey and serve warm.

SOURDOUGH ENTREES

Recipes include:

- Dumplings
- Country Fry Sourdough Batter
- Papa's Sourdough Noobles
- Sourdough Pizza Crust

Decades ago, sourdough was an equivalent to the American Express card--you didn't leave home without it. Inside a crock of zesty, bubbling sourdough batter was the potential for mouth-watering breads, biscuits, pancakes, even entrees, all while on the trail.

Nowadays, though, in an age of high tech equipment and quick to fix, dehydrated silver bag entrees like Turkey Tetrazzini, Beef Bourguignon and Cantonese Shrimp, who wants to deal with a messy bubbling ooze that smells like beer but isn't, and could blow up in your pack at any time unless properly stored? Who could possibly be crazy enough to pack a thing like sourdough? Me.

During our stint in Canada, Dave and I experimented with our choices for dinner entrees. Yes, we did bring our ration of high tech trail food, the choice of astronauts, tech weenies, and yuppies everywhere. Yes, trail food is convenient, light weight, easy to fix, relatively tasty, and we ate our share of it. But don't be fooled. We did not use trail food instead of sourdough, but *in addition to* sourdough which gave us some variety, and for that we're thankful. However, one package of trail food is only good for one meal, whereas one package of sourdough is good for hundreds of meals, generations of hungry bellies, and can choke starvation to death.

Entrees are usually associated with dinner. After a long hard day of trekking, or canoeing, the thought of a hardy flavored dinner is overwhelming. The choice of just the right entree is crucial. For Dave and me, pizza was usually the choice. We loved to whip up some sourdough pizza dough and make "ZA" anytime we were really feeling hungry. Pizza is usually well accepted among varied campers which makes it a good menu choice on trips. So be sure and try the pizza dough recipe on page 42.

DUMPLINGS

(RECIPE YIELDS 15 DUMPLINGS.)

1 cup flour
1 tsp. salt
1½ tsp. baking soda
¼ cup shortening
1½ cups primary batter
¼ cup milk or cream

Mix the ingredients in order, stirring as little as possible until the dough is soft. Scoop tablespoons of the dough and drop onto the top of the stew. Try to get the dumplings to stay afloat on top of the stew so they can rise. Cover the top quickly and don't open for 15 minutes or until done. Test for doneness by sticking the dumplings with a toothpick; if it comes out clean they are cooked.

COUNTRY FRY
SOURDOUGH BATTER

(RECIPE YIELDS ENOUGH BATTER FOR 2 POUNDS
OF MEAT, FISH, OR POULTRY.)

1 beaten egg

$\frac{1}{4}$ cup milk

1 tsp. poultry or fish seasoning

$\frac{1}{4}$ tsp. black pepper

1 tsp. salt

$\frac{1}{4}$ tsp. baking soda

1 cup primary batter

Mix the egg, milk and stir. Add the seasoning, black pepper, salt and stir well. Mix in baking soda and primary batter to the rest of the mixture and stir well. Cut up the meat, wash clean and drain. Place each piece into the batter covering all sides well. Place into a hot frying pan with about $1/2$ inch of oil. Cook each side until brown, cut heat to simmer and continue to cook for at least an additional 30 minutes, turning once meanwhile. Once done, drain and serve with mashed potatoes and gravy or sourdough biscuits and gravy.

PAPA'S SOURDOUGH NOOBLES

(RECIPE YIELDS 3 SERVINGS.)

* Please note: There is no type-o. It is "Noobles." He calls them "noobles." What can I say? Papa's a card. That's all.

1 cup primary batter

2 beaten eggs (or 2 cups of snow)

$\frac{1}{4}$ tsp. baking soda

$\frac{3}{4}$ tsp. salt

2 Tbs. melted butter

2-3 cups white flour

Mix ingredients well into a warm bowl. Add the flour $1/2$ cup at a time, mixing well until the dough is tough and will form a ball without sticking to the bowl. Put dough out onto a flat floured surface and divide into two pieces. Roll out each half very thin and be sure to keep the dough floured well while rolling. Cut dough into long strips about $1/2$ inch wide and then cut the strips into 2 inch pieces. Flour noobles again and place on a flat pan or baking sheet. Cook the noobles in boiling chicken or beef broth until tender. This should take about 15 to 20 minutes.

SOURDOUGH PIZZA CRUST
(RECIPE YIELDS ONE PIZZA CRUST.)

1 cup primary batter

1 tsp. sugar

1 tsp. salt

2 tsp. oil

1 cup flour (add more as needed)

Mix ingredients in order. Add additional flour if needed. Mix well until you have a thick, yet pliable dough. Roll into a ball and let the dough proof for thirty minutes. Then roll out your pizza dough, garnish it with all your favorite toppings or in some cases, with whatever you have available. Then bake at 350 degrees Fahrenheit for 20 minutes or until it's done.

In regard to toppings, use whatever you like. Mushrooms, sardines, rabbit, pineapple, oatmeal, squirrel, whatever. You can even forage for edible wild plants to top your pizza with. Make sure whatever you find is indeed edible. Otherwise you may jeopardize your health. For a reference, consult *The Basic Essentials of Edible Wild Plants* by Jim Meuninck, published by ICS Books, Inc., Merrillville, Indiana.

SOURDOUGH
FRENCH BREAD

Recipes include:
- French Bread
- French Rolls

First and foremost, don't get your hopes up to bake French bread that tastes like what you had while in San Francisco, it just won't happen. Why? Because the main ingredient can't be bought in any store, anywhere, not even in San Francisco. It's called *Lactobacillus sanfrancisco*, a bacterium exclusive to the Bay area. In San Fran, as the bread proofs a sugar called maltose is made. The bacterium uses the maltose to make lactic and acetic acids, seventy and thirty percent respectively. This gives the bread its sour flavor.

We must call a spade a spade. Even if we had *Lactobacillus sanfrancisco*, we still don't have the expertise and dedicated equipment necessary to produce the world famous sourdough French bread that the Bay City master bakers create. However, we must rise to the occasion of a backcountry French bread feast and put our best recipes to the test. And, if that doesn't work, there's an old fable that claims old-time bakers used to give the bread its special flavor by shaping the dough and making the loaves in their armpits. Try this and taste what happens. It may work. If all else fails, you may find out that your dough makes better deodorant.

FRENCH BREAD

(RECIPE YIELDS 2 LOAVES.)

1½ cups primary batter

1 cup warm water

2 tsp. salt

4 cups flour

Add the primary batter, the warm water (no hotter than 95 degrees), in a large bowl. Then stir in one cup of flour and spread salt on top of the batter. Mix in additional flour ½ cup at a time. While mixing, scrape the sides of the bowl so the dough doesn't stick. Use additional flour if necessary. Pour dough onto a well floured, flat surface and knead it until the dough is smooth and elastic, adding flour if needed. Place the dough in a large, warm bowl at least 4 quarts in capacity. Cover tightly with plastic wrap, and place in a warm spot for proofing. This should take two hours or until double in size.

Afterwards, knead dough on a lightly floured surface for about a minute, and divide the dough into two equal pieces. Fold each piece in half lengthwise, cover, and let rest for 5 minutes. Each piece can be shaped into a loaf by patting it out into a large oval about 1½ inches thick. Fold the loaf from back to front and seal the near edge with pinches. Roll the dough around so the seal is on the top. With your hands flatten the dough again and press a trench down the center of the oval with your fingers. Fold the pieces in half lengthwise again and seal the near edge again with pinches. Then roll the dough back and forth in the palms of your hands until it reaches a length about 2 inches shorter than your baking sheet.

Once the loaves are the right size, put them on a greased baking sheet which has been covered with white cornmeal. Be sure to place the loaves with the seam down and at least 3 inches apart from each other. Cover the loaves but don't let the covering touch the dough. Put in a warm place for proofing until double in bulk. This will probably take one hour after which the loaves are ready to bake, but first cut 3 diagonal slashes across the top of the loaves, then brush with cold water. The cuts and cold water help to give the crust its rough texture and golden color.

Before baking put a pan of water in the bottom of the preheated oven, this produces steam and helps brown the crust. Then bake the loaves in the oven at 400 degrees. After ten minutes of baking, remove the pan of water and continue to bake for 35 minutes or until the loaves are browned. Remove the bread and let cool on a wire rack. To add sheen to the crust brush with water. Avoid the temptation to eat the bread while it's hot and smells so good. French bread is not done baking until the bread has completely cooled. It tastes much better this way.

FRENCH ROLLS

(RECIPE YIELDS 15 ROLLS.)

1½ cups primary batter

1 cup warm water

2 tsp. salt

4 cups flour

Follow directions above for sourdough French bread until proofing is complete. Then after the dough has doubled in size turn dough onto a flat, floured surface and knead it for one minute. Then roll it out flat to a $1^{1/2}$ inch thickness, and with a sharp knife or cookie cutter cut the dough into 15 pieces each 4 inches square.

Fold each piece over itself and seal the edge with pinches. Put the rolls on a greased baking sheet that has been covered with white cornmeal. Place the rolls in rows about 3 inches apart. Cover the dough with a cloth but don't let it touch the rolls, and set them in a warm spot until double in bulk. Before baking, cut a lengthwise slash in each roll with a sharp knife and brush the rolls with cold water. Put a pan of boiling water on the bottom of the oven which should be preheated to 400 degrees. Place the rolls inside the oven. Bake for 15 minutes and remove the pan of water. Continue to bake the rolls for an additional 30 minutes or until golden brown. Remove and let cool on wire racks.

SOURDOUGH PANCAKES & WAFFLES

Recipes include:

- Apple Pancakes
- Bacon Pancakes
- Chocolate Waffles
- Cornmeal Pancakes
- Cornmeal Waffles
- Oat Pancakes
- Rice Pancakes
- Russian Pancakes
- Sourdough Waffles
- Traditional Sourdough Pancakes
- Whole Wheat Pancakes
- Whole Wheat Waffles

Pancakes were a big part of my wilderness diet. Really, when it came down to it, my options for breakfast were as limitless as my imagination. When I was hungry, and the need to be fed was greater than my want of a gourmet meal, I would whip up some oatmeal with tea or coffee. Otherwise, pancakes were prepared a couple of times a week, if not more.

It's quite a process to fix pancakes. I'd be a liar if I said it was a skill of instinct. In reality, the development of my ability to fix killer pancakes was only a direct result of the sacrificed lives of innocent pancakes, born prematurely to die of hyperthermia in the heat of the skillet.

Sourdough pancakes were a favorite to eat. They were the most filling and best tasting. In addition to all of that, the left-overs made great snacks or target practice, whichever you prefer. While living in the cabin, sourdough pancakes were also a favorite amongst neighboring squirrels, weasels, and Canadian Jays.

I'll never forget the time when I was awakened by a small pine squirrel that had managed to get himself into the loft where I was sleeping. The noise across the floor, as he scurried, disturbed me enough to open my eyes. He had entered the cabin through a small gap between a ceiling log and a wall log. He would come in early in the morning and search for scraps lying around. If scraps weren't available, he would try to open a box or bag of goodies himself. This morning however, he had managed to find one sourdough pancake leftover from the day before. Upon discovering that the pancake smelled better than pinecone seeds, the pine squirrel secured the cake between its jaws, and was en route to his nest with it when I noticed him.

First of all, I was in awe of the squirrel's ability to gracefully maneuver the pancake. I likened it to the way one would handle a priceless piece of art. To the squirrel, no doubt, the pancake was a priceless find, worthy of all the effort to keep it safe.

The squirrel was trying to take the pancake through the gap from which it had entered, but since the pancake was wider than the hole, the squirrel ran into a problem. When pushing with the pancake still in its mouth, the squirrel couldn't get the cake to fit through. Frustrated with perplexion, the squirrel put down the cake and began to stare at the gap and the pancake. How was he going to get this precious treasure through the hole?

Having determined a strategy, the squirrel bounded over the pancake and dashed into the gap, out of my sight. A second later, the squirrel stuck its head out, grabbed the cake between its jaws and *pulled* it through the hole. Success!

Well, fortunately we humans don't have to go through all of that for the mouth-watering, delicious flavor, and satisfaction of sourdough pancakes. All we have to do is follow the recipe, fry 'em till golden brown, and hope they'll fit in our mouths. If they do fit, let's hope they taste good too.

To ensure the flavor and overall success of your recipe it's important to keep some things in mind. For instance, the cooking technique for a pancake is different than the cooking technique for a waffle. The pancake cooking technique is as follows: Take a spoon full of pancake batter and place it onto a hot, lightly greased skillet. Place the cakes sparsely so that they do not touch. Fry the cakes until air bubbles begin to appear on the top side of the cake. When this happens, take a spatula and slide it under the edges of the pancake and lift it just enough to look underneath and see if the bottom is browned and done frying. If so, flip the pancake and fry the other side until it's browned as well. The most important thing when frying pancakes is to be patient and wait until the pancake is done frying before you try to flip it. Otherwise, you'll end up with a gooey mess inside your skillet and your fellow campers may lose their appetites.

Preparing waffles is a different process and may be easier for you than cooking pancakes. The main difference is the cooking utensil; waffles are made in a waffle iron. These can be purchased at your local camping outfitter, sporting goods store, K-Mart, or Wal-Mart. Simply place the batter inside a preheated waffle iron and cook until steam appears. Open the waffle iron to check for doneness. If the waffles don't stick and are golden brown, they are done. Flip them out and serve.

APPLE PANCAKES

(RECIPE YIELDS 8 2-INCH CAKES.)

$1\frac{1}{2}$ cups primary batter

1 cup flour

2 eggs or two cups snow

3 Tbs. sugar

2 Tbs. melted butter

1 tsp. salt

$\frac{1}{2}$ cup milk

1 cup sliced apples

1 tsp. nutmeg

1 tsp. vanilla

Mix ingredients in succession. Let batter rest for 10 minutes. Spoon each cake onto a preheated, lightly greased skillet. Fry until the top glazes over and the surface no longer appears shiny, then flip. The bottom should be a perfect golden brown. Once both sides are browned, serve hot with peanut butter and honey.

BACON PANCAKES

(RECIPE YIELDS 4 3-INCH CAKES.)

$1\frac{1}{2}$ cups primary batter

1 cup flour

2 eggs or two cups snow

3 Tbs. sugar

2 Tbs. melted butter

1 tsp. salt

$\frac{1}{2}$ cup milk

6-8 fried bacon slices crumbled

Mix ingredients in order. Let batter rest for 10 minutes. Spoon each cake onto a preheated, lightly greased skillet. Fry until the bottom is browned, then flip. Once both sides are browned, serve hot with toppings of your choice. HINT: For a stronger bacon taste, crumble a little bacon into the pancake syrup or other topping.

CHOCOLATE WAFFLES

(RECIPE YIELDS 3 6-INCH SQUARE WAFFLES.)

$1\frac{1}{2}$ cups primary batter

2 eggs

3 Tbs. sugar

$\frac{1}{2}$ tsp. salt

$\frac{1}{2}$ cup cocoa

$\frac{1}{2}$ tsp. vanilla

$\frac{1}{2}$ cup butter

1 cup milk

Mix ingredients in succession. Pour batter onto a preheated waffle iron. Cook waffles in iron until steam disappears. If waffles are golden brown, stick a fork in them because they're done. Serve hot with toppings such as whipped cream and chocolate syrup.

CORNMEAL PANCAKES
(RECIPE YIELDS 10 2-INCH PANCAKES.)

1½ cups primary batter

2 eggs or two cups snow

3 Tbs. sugar

2 Tbs. melted butter

1 tsp. salt

1 cup milk

1 cup yellow cornmeal

Mix ingredients in order. Let batter set for 10 minutes. Spoon each cake onto a preheated, lightly greased skillet. Fry until the bottom is browned, then flip. Once both sides are browned, serve hot with your favorite toppings.

CORNMEAL WAFFLES
(RECIPE YIELDS 3 6-INCH SQUARE WAFFLES.)

1½ cups primary batter

½ cup milk

3 eggs

3 tsp. sugar

½ tsp. salt

¼ cup butter

1 cup cornmeal

Mix ingredients in succession. Pour batter onto a preheated waffle iron. Cook waffles in iron until steam disappears. If waffles are golden brown, they're done. Serve hot with toppings such as honey, maple syrup, or jam.

OAT PANCAKES
(RECIPE YIELDS 15 2-INCH CAKES.)

1½ cups primary batter

2 eggs or two cups snow

3 Tbs. sugar

2 Tbs. melted butter or margarine

1½ tsp. salt

1 cup milk

1 cup oats

Mix ingredients in succession. Let batter rest for 10 minutes. Spoon each cake onto a preheated, lightly greased skillet. Fry until the bottom is browned, then flip. Once both sides are browned, serve hot with toppings of your choice. Maple syrup is my favorite for this dish.

RICE PANCAKES
(RECIPE YIELDS 4 3-INCH CAKES.)

1½ cups primary batter

1 cup flour

2 eggs or two cups snow

3 Tbs. sugar

2 Tbs. melted butter

1 tsp. salt

½ cup milk

½ cup cooked rice

½ tsp. vanilla

Mix ingredients. Let batter set for 10 minutes. Spoon each cake onto a preheated, lightly greased skillet. Fry until the bottom is browned, then flip. Once both sides are browned, serve hot with butter and honey.

RUSSIAN PANCAKES
(RECIPE YIELDS 15 RUSSIAN PANCAKES.)

1 cup primary batter

1 Tbs. sugar

¼ cup milk

2 eggs beaten or two cups snow

1 tsp. baking soda

½ tsp. salt

½ cup flour

2 Tbs. butter

Mix ingredients consecutively. Let batter stand for 10 minutes. Melt 2 Tbs. butter in skillet and fry pancakes small.

SOURDOUGH WAFFLES
(RECIPE YIELDS 3 6-INCH SQUARE WAFFLES.)

1½ cups primary batter

2 eggs

3 tsp. sugar

½ tsp. salt

¼ cup melted butter

¼ cup milk

Mix ingredients in order. Pour batter into a preheated waffle iron. Cook waffles in iron until steam disappears. If waffles are golden brown, they're done. Serve hot with toppings such as honey, maple syrup, or jam.

TRADITIONAL SOURDOUGH PANCAKES
(RECIPE YIELDS 5 LARGE PANCAKES.)

$1\frac{1}{2}$ cups primary batter

$\frac{1}{2}$ cup white flour

1 egg or one cup snow

1 Tbs. sugar

1 Tbs. melted butter

$\frac{3}{4}$ tsp. salt

2 Tbs. milk

Mix ingredients in succession. Let batter rest for 10 minutes. Spoon each cake onto a preheated, lightly greased skillet. Fry until the bottom is browned, then flip. Once both sides are browned, serve hot with toppings of your choice. Butter and honey are my favorite.

WHOLE WHEAT PANCAKES
(RECIPE YIELDS 5 LARGE PANCAKES.)

$1\frac{1}{2}$ cups primary batter

2 eggs or two cups snow

2 Tbs. sugar

2 Tbs. melted butter

1 tsp. salt

$\frac{1}{2}$ cup milk

1 cup whole wheat flour

Mix ingredients consecutively. Let batter set for 10 minutes. Spoon each cake onto a preheated, lightly greased, skillet. Fry until the bottom is browned, then flip. Once both sides are browned, serve hot with toppings of your choice.

WHOLE WHEAT WAFFLES

(RECIPE YIELDS 3 6-INCH SQUARE WAFFLES.)

1½ cups primary batter

½ cup milk

2 eggs separated

3 tsp. sugar

½ tsp. salt

¼ cup melted butter

½ cup whole wheat flour

Mix ingredients in succession. Pour batter onto a preheated waffle iron. Cook waffles in iron until steam disappears. If waffles are golden brown, stick a fork in them because they're done. Serve hot with your best toppings.

TOP TEN MISCELLANEOUS USES OF SOURDOUGH

Besides delicious pancakes, breads, desserts and entrees, sourdough leads another life of miscellaneous uses. Sourdough is an epicurean double agent, posing as a simple leavener, when in reality it is a complex organism that plays many roles.

The top ten miscellaneous uses of sourdough, are:

10. Beer

It is possible to make sourdough beer that will get you drunk if you can stand to drink it. The recipe is this: Mix 3 cups of rice, berries, or barley (any fruit or grain will do) with 4 cups sugar, three cups sourdough batter and two gallons of warm water. Let set for five days in a warm, dry place to ferment. Then bottoms up!

9. Glue

Sourdough, once allowed to dry will harden like cement. This makes it a great bonding agent. At the cabin, sourdough has been used many times to repair broken wooden objects such as the spatula and chairs.

8. Gift

Sourdough makes a great gift. It represents the gift of food which ensures health and sustains life and that's the best kind of gift there is. Our sourdough crock and starter kit was given to Dave and I before we went to the cabin. It fed us and sustained us and gave us much pleasure.

7. Stain removal tester

If you're considering buying a stain remover like those you see for carpets, clothing, et hoc genus omne, and are having a hard time deciding which one is the best, try this: Take some sourdough batter and smear it all over the sale clerk's jacket. (With their permission of course.) Let it dry until hardened. Then use the stain remover in question to try and remove the sourdough stain. Whichever one works, buy it. However, what you may find is that the stain is impossible to remove from the jacket, and you may end up having to buy the clerk a new jacket. Because, in my experience, once sourdough has a chance to dry itself onto something it is impossible to remove.

6. Incense

Sourdough is very aromatic. It fills the room with its beer-like aroma just like burning incense does.

5. Mouse trap

If you're having problems with mice invading camp and forgot to bring the traps, just place little piles of sourdough batter strategically so that the mice will find it, wander into it, and get stuck like victims in quick sand.

4. Weapon

Figure that one out for yourself, I hate violence.

3. Family heirloom

Back during the sourdough craze, and in the country where food was sometimes scarce, it was very normal for families to pass crocks of sourdough starter from generation to generation. It was the most valued and precious possession in the household.

2. Caulk

Sourdough is great to fill those little holes around the cabin window that the winds of winter seem to love.

1. Food fights

Self-explanatory.

So you see, sourdough is more than meets the eye, or even the mouth. It is the chameleon of cookery, the "Breakfast of Champions" mentor, the tour de force of flavor, the wind in your sails, the spring in your step, the hip in your hop, your sunshine your only sunshine and happiness when skies are grey, the candle under your bushel, the pickle in your pocket, your nutritional safety belt and helmet from hunger. Use it.

APPENDICES

TRAIL STOVE MAINTENANCE AND TIPS

The most practical trail stoves for cooking in the outdoors are not necessarily those that burn the hottest or are most expensive. Use these guidelines as a basis for stove selection.

1. Stove stability is important. Avoid stoves that threaten to topple. Look for a low-to-the-ground profile.

2. Ease-of-starting: Some stoves come equipped with pumps for easier starting and more efficient use in cold weather. Stay away from stoves that require considerable pumping to start or maintain flame.

3. Wind susceptibility: First time you have to build a rock wall around your stove to keep it perking in the wind, you'll understand the importance of a good windscreen. Avoid aluminum foil windscreens that interfere with the use of skillet handles.

4. High heat output: For winter cooking you need blow-torch performance. A winter stove should boil a quart of water (at sea level) in an uncovered pot in less than five minutes. If you want efficiency, stick with stoves that burn white gas or propane (if you can carry the heavy fuel tanks). The efficiency of butane is directly proportional to heat and altitude. In below freezing weather, butane stoves don't work at all. On mountain tops, because of the low air pressure, they work fine. The typical butane stove requires at least eight minutes to boil a quart of water at 70 degrees Fahrenheit, at sea level. Kerosene stoves burn hot and are very safe (they can't explode). However, kerosene is oily and smelly--the reason why it's unpopular. But if you're traveling in Europe, where white gas is unavailable, kerosene is the logical choice.

5. Simmering heat: High heat output is great, but so is a low-simmering flame. Some of the best winter stoves (like the MSR X-GK) are not adjustable enough for gourmet cooking.

6. Weight: Some of the most reliable and versatile trail stoves are relatively heavy by backpacking standards. Examples include the Optimus 111B and 111 Hiker, the Phoenix Mountaineer, and the venerable Coleman twin burner.

7. Ruggedness: If a part looks weak, it probably is. If there's a plastic knob which can burn or break, it will. If there are components which may be lost, count on it. The best trail stoves are rugged, compact, and have no parts to break, burn, assemble or lose.

8. Gasoline or multi-fuel?: Get a multi-fuel stove only if you need it. Multi-fuel stoves don't burn as hot as equivalent gas models and they are much more expensive.

STOVE MAINTENANCE TIPS

1. For greatest efficiency and trouble-free operation, use Coleman or Blazo fuel (it's naphtha, not white gas) in your gasoline stove. These pre-filtered fuels burn clean and have extremely high heat output.

2. Don't fill gasoline stoves more than three-fourths full. You need air space to generate pressure.

3. Empty the fuel from your stove after each trip. And, burn dry what you can't pour out. Fuel left in stoves leaves varnishes which clog jets and filters--the major reason for stove failure!

4. Once a year (if you use your stove a lot) add a capful--no more--of Gumout Carburetor Cleaner to your stove along with a half tank of gas. Burn the stove dry. The Gumout will dissolve built-up varnishes.

5. Keep your stove in a fabric sack when it's not in use. This will prevent dust and debris from getting into the working parts.

6. Lubricate leather pump washers with high temperature gun oil. Avoid use of multi-purpose and vegetable oils which may break down and gum up valves.

COMMON WEIGHTS
AND USEFUL MEASUREMENTS

3 teaspoons	is equivalent to	1 Tablespoon
2 Tablespoons	is equivalent to	1 liquid ounce
16 Tablespoons	is equivalent to	1 cup
1 cup	is equivalent to	8 ounces
2 cups	is equivalent to	1 pint
4 cups	is equivalent to	1 quart

No. 10 can holds about 12 cups of water.

1 level full Sierra cup holds a little more than 1 cup water.

1 standard sized plastic insulated cup holds about $1\frac{1}{3}$ cups water.

$\frac{1}{2}$ lb. margarine	is equivalent to	1 cup
1 lb. of granulated sugar	is equivalent to	2 cups
1 lb. of brown sugar	is equivalent to	3 cups
1 cup chopped nuts	is equivalent to	about $\frac{1}{2}$ lb.
64 marshmallows	is equivalent to	1 lb.
1 medium onion	is equivalent to	2 Tablespoons of minced dry onions

1 Tablespoon of fresh herbs = $\frac{1}{2}$ teaspoon of dried herbs, or $\frac{1}{4}$ teaspoon of dried, powdered herbs.

1 cup sour milk = 1 cup milk into which 1 Tablespoon vinegar has been stirred.

1 cup sour cream can be made by adding $\frac{1}{3}$ cup butter, $\frac{2}{3}$ cup milk, and 1 Tablespoon vinegar.

Butter or margarine: 1 oz.	is equivalent to	2 Tbs fat
$\frac{1}{4}$ lb. or 1 stick	is equivalent to	$\frac{1}{2}$ cup fat
$\frac{1}{2}$ lb.	is equivalent to	1 cup fat
1 lb.	is equivalent to	2 cups fat
Chocolate: 1 square	is equivalent to	1 oz. = $3\frac{1}{2}$ Tbs. dry cocoa + 1 Tbs. butter
Eggs: 1 cup snow	is equivalent to	1 egg
13 egg yolks	is equivalent to	1 cup
9 egg whites	is equivalent to	1 cup
Flour: 1 lb. All-purpose sifted	is equivalent to	4 cups
1 lb. cake flour	is equivalent to	$4\frac{1}{2}$ cups
1 lb. cornmeal	is equivalent to	3 cups
Rice: 1 lb.	is equivalent to	$2\frac{1}{3}$ cups uncooked rice
Sugar: 1 lb. granulated	is equivalent to	2 cups
1 lb. brown	is equivalent to	3 cups
1 lb. confectionery	is equivalent to	$3\frac{1}{2}$ cups

Epilogue

Much time has past since I began writing COOKING THE SOUR-DOUGH WAY by candlelight at the cabin, yet it seems just like moments ago. I think back to those days and know they were special beyond words. Yet, using words, I often try and explain to people like yourself some of those moments that Dave Scott and I saw (Aurora Borealis), heard (silence), felt (60 below zero), tasted (sourdough pancakes), and smelled (spring). But, it's difficult. Skill is needed. One must use words very effectively to convey the sensation of experience and the reality of the moment.

Unfortunately, you were not there with Dave and me at the cabin, counting hundreds of bug bites on a July afternoon, watching the boiling spectrum of Northern Lights that fill the night sky, freezing with frost bite at 60 below zero. Unfortunately, you were not there with Dave and me at the cabin. Therefore, it is impossible for you to know what it was really like. Often times, Dave and I will call each other on the phone to reminisce, saying, "Remember when . . ." and we are the only two people in the whole world who can remember. So, this is why we must use words to help record and explain the adventure, mystery, and romance of our wilderness refuge.

Within these pages, I have tried to write those words that might cause you to learn something you can use and enjoy. I hope I've succeeded. But, if there is a person who can compose words to best transport you, the reader, to that little rustic cabin I love so much it would be my partner, Dave Scott. So, with a delicate touch and the precision of a surgeon Dave has written *Paridise Creek* (ICS Books). Not just another published journal of some distant adventure, but a heart felt look at two young men as they travel a rite of passage from the status quo of civilization to the beautiful, yet dangerous, wilderness of northern Canada. I hope you can obtain a copy and read it while you eat some sourdough bread.

INDEX